Daily
Student
Planner
Book Club

This Planner Belongs To:

____

____

Daily Student Planner

M   T   W   T   F

Priorities

-
-
-

today's schedule :

07.00

08.00

09.00

10.00

11.00

12.00

13.00

14.00

Assignment :

notes :

Daily Student Planner

M T W T F

Priorities

-
-
-

Assignment :

today's schedule :

07.00

08.00

09.00

10.00

11.00

12.00

13.00

14.00

notes :

Daily Student Planner

M T W T F

Priorities

- ⬤
- ⬤
- ⬤

Assignment :

today's schedule :

07.00

08.00

09.00

10.00

11.00

12.00

13.00

14.00

notes :

Daily Student Planner

M   T   W   T   F

Priorities

-
-
-

Assignment :

today's schedule :

07.00

08.00

09.00

10.00

11.00

12.00

13.00

14.00

notes :

Daily Student Planner

M T W T F

Priorities

-
-
-

Assignment :

today's schedule :

07.00

08.00

09.00

10.00

11.00

12.00

13.00

14.00

notes :

Daily Student Planner

M T W T F

Priorities

-
-
-

today's schedule :

07.00

08.00

09.00

10.00

11.00

12.00

13.00

14.00

Assignment :

notes :

Daily Student Planner

M T W T F

Priorities

-
-
-

today's schedule :

07.00

08.00

09.00

10.00

11.00

12.00

13.00

14.00

Assignment :

notes :

Daily Student Planner

M T W T F

Priorities

-
-
-

Assignment :

today's schedule :

07.00

08.00

09.00

10.00

11.00

12.00

13.00

14.00

notes :

Daily Student Planner

Priorities

-
-
-

Assignment :

today's schedule :

07.00

08.00

09.00

10.00

11.00

12.00

13.00

14.00

notes :

Daily Student Planner

M T W T F

Priorities

today's schedule :

07.00

08.00

09.00

10.00

11.00

12.00

13.00

14.00

Assignment :

notes :

Daily Student Planner

M T W T F

Priorities

today's schedule :

07.00

08.00

09.00

10.00

11.00

12.00

13.00

14.00

Assignment :

notes :

Daily Student Planner

Priorities

today's schedule :

07.00

08.00

09.00

10.00

11.00

12.00

13.00

14.00

Assignment :

notes :

Daily Student Planner

M T W T F

Priorities

today's schedule :

07.00

08.00

09.00

10.00

11.00

12.00

13.00

14.00

Assignment :

notes :

Daily Student Planner

M T W T F

Priorities

- ●
- ●
- ●

Assignment :

today's schedule :

07.00

08.00

09.00

10.00

11.00

12.00

13.00

14.00

notes :

Daily Student Planner

M   T   W   T   F

Priorities

today's schedule :

07.00

08.00

09.00

10.00

11.00

12.00

13.00

14.00

Assignment :

notes :

Daily Student Planner

M T W T F

Priorities

today's schedule :

07.00

08.00

09.00

10.00

11.00

12.00

13.00

14.00

Assignment :

notes :

Daily Student Planner

M   T   W   T   F

Priorities

today's schedule :

07.00

08.00

09.00

10.00

11.00

12.00

13.00

14.00

Assignment :

notes :

Daily Student Planner

M T W T F

Priorities

-
-
-

Assignment :

today's schedule :

07.00

08.00

09.00

10.00

11.00

12.00

13.00

14.00

notes :

Daily Student Planner

M T W T F

Priorities

today's schedule :

07.00

08.00

09.00

10.00

11.00

12.00

13.00

14.00

Assignment :

notes :

Daily Student Planner

Priorities

today's schedule :

07.00

08.00

09.00

10.00

11.00

12.00

13.00

14.00

Assignment :

notes :

Daily Student Planner

M T W T F

Priorities

today's schedule :

07.00

08.00

09.00

10.00

11.00

12.00

13.00

14.00

Assignment :

notes :

Daily Student Planner

M T W T F

Priorities

Assignment :

today's schedule :

07.00

08.00

09.00

10.00

11.00

12.00

13.00

14.00

notes :

Daily Student Planner

M T W T F

Priorities

today's schedule :

07.00

08.00

09.00

10.00

11.00

12.00

13.00

14.00

Assignment :

notes :

Daily Student Planner

M T W T F

Priorities

- ●
- ●
- ●

Assignment :

today's schedule :

07.00

08.00

09.00

10.00

11.00

12.00

13.00

14.00

notes :

Daily Student Planner

M T W T F

Priorities

-
-
-

today's schedule :

07.00

08.00

09.00

10.00

11.00

12.00

13.00

14.00

Assignment :

notes :

Daily Student Planner

M   T   W   T   F

Priorities

-
-
-

today's schedule :

07.00

08.00

09.00

10.00

11.00

12.00

13.00

14.00

Assignment :

notes :

Daily Student Planner

M T W T F

Priorities

-
-
-

Assignment :

today's schedule :

07.00

08.00

09.00

10.00

11.00

12.00

13.00

14.00

notes :

Daily Student Planner

M T W T F

Priorities

today's schedule :

07.00

08.00

09.00

10.00

11.00

12.00

13.00

14.00

Assignment :

notes :

Daily Student Planner

M T W T F

Priorities

-
-
-

today's schedule :

07.00

08.00

09.00

10.00

11.00

12.00

13.00

14.00

Assignment :

notes :

Daily Student Planner

M T W T F

Priorities

-
-
-

Assignment :

today's schedule :

07.00

08.00

09.00

10.00

11.00

12.00

13.00

14.00

notes :

Daily Student Planner

M T W T F

Priorities

today's schedule :

07.00

08.00

09.00

10.00

11.00

12.00

13.00

14.00

Assignment :

notes :

Daily Student Planner

M T W T F

Priorities

-
-
-

Assignment :

today's schedule :

07.00

08.00

09.00

10.00

11.00

12.00

13.00

14.00

notes :

Daily Student Planner

Priorities

-
-
-

Assignment :

today's schedule :

07.00

08.00

09.00

10.00

11.00

12.00

13.00

14.00

notes :

Daily Student Planner

M T W T F

Priorities

Assignment :

today's schedule :

07.00

08.00

09.00

10.00

11.00

12.00

13.00

14.00

notes :

Daily Student Planner

M T W T F

Priorities

today's schedule :

07.00

08.00

09.00

10.00

11.00

12.00

13.00

14.00

Assignment :

notes :

Daily Student Planner

M T W T F

Priorities

-
-
-

Assignment :

today's schedule :

07.00

08.00

09.00

10.00

11.00

12.00

13.00

14.00

notes :

Daily Student Planner

M T W T F

Priorities

today's schedule :

07.00

08.00

09.00

10.00

11.00

12.00

13.00

14.00

Assignment :

notes :

Daily Student Planner

M T W T F

Priorities

-
-
-

Assignment :

today's schedule :

07.00

08.00

09.00

10.00

11.00

12.00

13.00

14.00

notes :

Daily Student Planner

M T W T F

Priorities

today's schedule :

07.00

08.00

09.00

10.00

11.00

12.00

13.00

14.00

Assignment :

notes :

Daily Student Planner

M T W T F

Priorities

today's schedule :

07.00

08.00

09.00

10.00

11.00

12.00

13.00

14.00

Assignment :

notes :

Daily Student Planner

M T W T F

Priorities

-
-
-

Assignment :

today's schedule :

07.00

08.00

09.00

10.00

11.00

12.00

13.00

14.00

notes :

Daily Student Planner

M T W T F

Priorities

- ⬤
- ⬤
- ⬤

Assignment :

today's schedule :

07.00

08.00

09.00

10.00

11.00

12.00

13.00

14.00

notes :

Daily Student Planner

M T W T F

Priorities

today's schedule :

07.00

08.00

09.00

10.00

11.00

12.00

13.00

14.00

Assignment :

notes :

Daily Student Planner

M T W T F

Priorities

Assignment :

today's schedule :

07.00

08.00

09.00

10.00

11.00

12.00

13.00

14.00

notes :

Daily Student Planner

Priorities

today's schedule :

07.00

08.00

09.00

10.00

11.00

12.00

13.00

14.00

Assignment :

notes :

Daily Student Planner

M T W T F

Priorities

today's schedule :

07.00

08.00

09.00

10.00

11.00

12.00

13.00

14.00

Assignment :

notes :

Daily Student Planner

M T W T F

Priorities

Assignment :

today's schedule :

07.00

08.00

09.00

10.00

11.00

12.00

13.00

14.00

notes :

Daily Student Planner

M   T   W   T   F

Priorities

-
-
-

Assignment :

today's schedule :

07.00

08.00

09.00

10.00

11.00

12.00

13.00

14.00

notes :

Daily Student Planner

M T W T F

Priorities

today's schedule :

07.00

08.00

09.00

10.00

11.00

12.00

13.00

14.00

Assignment :

notes :

Daily Student Planner

M T W T F

Priorities

-
-
-

Assignment :

today's schedule :

07.00

08.00

09.00

10.00

11.00

12.00

13.00

14.00

notes :

Daily Student Planner

M T W T F

Priorities

today's schedule :

07.00

08.00

09.00

10.00

11.00

12.00

13.00

14.00

Assignment :

notes :

Daily Student Planner

Priorities

-
-
-

Assignment :

today's schedule :

07.00

08.00

09.00

10.00

11.00

12.00

13.00

14.00

notes :

Daily Student Planner

M T W T F

Priorities

-
-
-

today's schedule :

07.00

08.00

09.00

10.00

11.00

12.00

13.00

14.00

Assignment :

notes :

Daily Student Planner

M   T   W   T   F

Priorities

- ○
- ○
- ○

Assignment :

today's schedule :

07.00

08.00

09.00

10.00

11.00

12.00

13.00

14.00

notes :

Daily Student Planner

M T W T F

Priorities

-
-
-

today's schedule :

07.00

08.00

09.00

10.00

11.00

12.00

13.00

14.00

Assignment :

notes :

Daily Student Planner

M T W T F

Priorities

today's schedule :

07.00

08.00

09.00

10.00

11.00

12.00

13.00

14.00

Assignment :

notes :

Daily Student Planner

M T W T F

Priorities

today's schedule :

07.00

08.00

09.00

10.00

11.00

12.00

13.00

14.00

Assignment :

notes :

Daily Student Planner

M T W T F

Priorities

- ●
- ●
- ●

Assignment :

today's schedule :

07.00

08.00

09.00

10.00

11.00

12.00

13.00

14.00

notes :

Daily Student Planner

M T W T F

Priorities

-
-
-

today's schedule :

07.00

08.00

09.00

10.00

11.00

12.00

13.00

14.00

Assignment :

notes :

Daily Student Planner

M T W T F

Priorities

Assignment :

today's schedule :

07.00

08.00

09.00

10.00

11.00

12.00

13.00

14.00

notes :

Daily Student Planner

M T W T F

Priorities

Assignment :

today's schedule :

07.00

08.00

09.00

10.00

11.00

12.00

13.00

14.00

notes :

Daily Student Planner

M T W T F

Priorities

-
-
-

today's schedule :

07.00

08.00

09.00

10.00

11.00

12.00

13.00

14.00

Assignment :

notes :

Daily Student Planner

M T W T F

Priorities

-
-
-

Assignment :

today's schedule :

07.00

08.00

09.00

10.00

11.00

12.00

13.00

14.00

notes :

Daily Student Planner

M T W T F

Priorities

-
-
-

Assignment :

today's schedule :

07.00

08.00

09.00

10.00

11.00

12.00

13.00

14.00

notes :

Daily Student Planner

M T W T F

Priorities

today's schedule :

07.00

08.00

09.00

10.00

11.00

12.00

13.00

14.00

Assignment :

notes :

Daily Student Planner

M T W T F

Priorities

-
-
-

today's schedule :

07.00

08.00

09.00

10.00

11.00

12.00

13.00

14.00

Assignment :

notes :

Daily Student Planner

M T W T F

Priorities

-
-
-

today's schedule :

07.00

08.00

09.00

10.00

11.00

12.00

13.00

14.00

Assignment :

notes :

Daily Student Planner

M T W T F

Priorities

today's schedule :

07.00

08.00

09.00

10.00

11.00

12.00

13.00

14.00

Assignment :

notes :

Daily Student Planner

M T W T F

Priorities

today's schedule :

07.00

08.00

09.00

10.00

11.00

12.00

13.00

14.00

Assignment :

notes :

Daily Student Planner

M T W T F

Priorities

Assignment :

today's schedule :

07.00

08.00

09.00

10.00

11.00

12.00

13.00

14.00

notes :

Daily Student Planner

M T W T F

Priorities

today's schedule :

07.00

08.00

09.00

10.00

11.00

12.00

13.00

14.00

Assignment :

notes :

Daily Student Planner

M T W T F

Priorities

today's schedule :

07.00

08.00

09.00

10.00

11.00

12.00

13.00

14.00

Assignment :

notes :

Daily Student Planner

M T W T F

Priorities

-
-
-

Assignment :

today's schedule :

07.00

08.00

09.00

10.00

11.00

12.00

13.00

14.00

notes :

Daily Student Planner

M T W T F

Priorities

today's schedule :

07.00

08.00

09.00

10.00

11.00

12.00

13.00

14.00

Assignment :

notes :

Daily Student Planner

M T W T F

Priorities

-
-
-

Assignment :

today's schedule :

07.00

08.00

09.00

10.00

11.00

12.00

13.00

14.00

notes :

Daily Student Planner

M   T   W   T   F

Priorities

-
-
-

Assignment :

today's schedule :

07.00

08.00

09.00

10.00

11.00

12.00

13.00

14.00

notes :

Daily Student Planner

M T W T F

Priorities

Assignment :

today's schedule :

07.00

08.00

09.00

10.00

11.00

12.00

13.00

14.00

notes :

Daily Student Planner

M T W T F

Priorities

- ●
- ●
- ●

Assignment :

today's schedule :

07.00

08.00

09.00

10.00

11.00

12.00

13.00

14.00

notes :

Daily Student Planner

Priorities

-
-
-

Assignment :

today's schedule :

07.00

08.00

09.00

10.00

11.00

12.00

13.00

14.00

notes :

Daily Student Planner

M T W T F

Priorities

- ●
- ●
- ●

Assignment :

today's schedule :

07.00

08.00

09.00

10.00

11.00

12.00

13.00

14.00

notes :

Daily Student Planner

Priorities

today's schedule :

07.00

08.00

09.00

10.00

11.00

12.00

13.00

14.00

Assignment :

notes :

Daily Student Planner

M T W T F

Priorities

Assignment :

today's schedule :

07.00

08.00

09.00

10.00

11.00

12.00

13.00

14.00

notes :

Daily Student Planner

M T W T F

Priorities

today's schedule :

07.00

08.00

09.00

10.00

11.00

12.00

13.00

14.00

Assignment :

notes :

Daily Student Planner

M T W T F

Priorities

-
-
-

Assignment :

today's schedule :

07.00

08.00

09.00

10.00

11.00

12.00

13.00

14.00

notes :

Daily Student Planner

M T W T F

Priorities

today's schedule :

07.00

08.00

09.00

10.00

11.00

12.00

13.00

14.00

Assignment :

notes :

Daily Student Planner

M T W T F

Priorities

Assignment :

today's schedule :

07.00

08.00

09.00

10.00

11.00

12.00

13.00

14.00

notes :

Daily Student Planner

M T W T F

Priorities

today's schedule :

07.00

08.00

09.00

10.00

11.00

12.00

13.00

14.00

Assignment :

notes :

Daily Student Planner

M T W T F

Priorities

today's schedule :

07.00

08.00

09.00

10.00

11.00

12.00

13.00

14.00

Assignment :

notes :

Daily Student Planner

M   T   W   T   F

Priorities

Assignment :

today's schedule :

07.00

08.00

09.00

10.00

11.00

12.00

13.00

14.00

notes :

Daily Student Planner

M T W T F

Priorities

-
-
-

Assignment :

today's schedule :

07.00

08.00

09.00

10.00

11.00

12.00

13.00

14.00

notes :

Daily Student Planner

M T W T F

Priorities

today's schedule :

07.00

08.00

09.00

10.00

11.00

12.00

13.00

14.00

Assignment :

notes :

Daily Student Planner

M T W T F

Priorities

today's schedule :

07.00

08.00

09.00

10.00

11.00

12.00

13.00

14.00

Assignment :

notes :

Daily Student Planner

M   T   W   T   F

Priorities

-
-
-

today's schedule :

07.00

08.00

09.00

10.00

11.00

12.00

13.00

14.00

Assignment :

notes :

Daily Student Planner

M   T   W   T   F

Priorities

today's schedule :

07.00

08.00

09.00

10.00

11.00

12.00

13.00

14.00

Assignment :

notes :

Daily Student Planner

Priorities

- ●
- ●
- ●

Assignment :

today's schedule :

07.00

08.00

09.00

10.00

11.00

12.00

13.00

14.00

notes :

Daily Student Planner

M T W T F

Priorities

today's schedule :

07.00

08.00

09.00

10.00

11.00

12.00

13.00

14.00

Assignment :

notes :

Daily Student Planner

M T W T F

Priorities

today's schedule :

07.00

08.00

09.00

10.00

11.00

12.00

13.00

14.00

Assignment :

notes :

Daily Student Planner

M T W T F

Priorities

-
-
-

today's schedule :

07.00

08.00

09.00

10.00

11.00

12.00

13.00

14.00

Assignment :

notes :

Daily Student Planner

M T W T F

Priorities

-
-
-

today's schedule :

07.00

08.00

09.00

10.00

11.00

12.00

13.00

14.00

Assignment :

notes :

Daily
Student
Planner
Book Club